From Flat Rock to Heaven

A Collection of Poetry and Short Stories

BY ARNOLD R. FAW

DORRANCE
PUBLISHING CO
EST. 1920
PITTSBURGH, PENNSYLVANIA 15238

Dorrance Publishing Co
585 Alpha Drive
Pittsburgh, PA 15238
Visit our website at *www.dorrancebookstore.com*

ISBN: 978-1-6376-4306-8
eISBN: 978-1-6376-4620-5

Book Dedication

With a grateful heart, I dedicate this book to the three wonderful ladies God placed in my life to provide inspiration, guidance, support, and love.

To the loving memory of my dear mother, Lillian Bowman Faw, who departed this life in 1991.

And, my deceased wife of thirty-three years, Linda Draughn Faw, who passed away in 1997. Also, my wife of the past nineteen years, Lynn Pugh Faw.

Truly, they were each a God-send to me. Each one has filled a phase of my life that would have been empty without them. We shared so much together. I am so blessed by each of them. May God give them a great reward in heaven.

Painting by Allysia Trindade.

LEAVING HERE

I eased into his bedroom, pulled up a chair, and sat down by his bed. I looked into his pale face and thought to myself, it won't be long now. I sat quietly for a while, then I took his hand in mine. He opened his eyes, and it seemed to me that he gathered up about all the strength he had left. He propped himself up on his elbow, and a smile broke across his face. Then, I saw a little glimmer in his eyes.

In a voice, as strong as I've ever heard him speak, he said,"Last night I dreamed I stood on the banks of old Jordan River. The Devil himself walked up to me and said, 'Whatcha got in the box, boy?' I said, 'I just knew you were going to be here; that I would have one more battle with you before I leave this world. You've been dogging my trail for more than half a century now. But, it ends right here, Devil. I'm on my way out of here, and you can't follow me where I'm going!'

"You asked what's in the box. These are the things I've collected during my journey on this earth. But, I'm done with them, and they're not allowed over yonder. So, I boxed them all up and brought them down here. I'm going to leave them with you. In fact, they're yours for ever more. Now, you can do whatever you want with them. You can throw them in that muddy old river, you can take them to hell with you, I really don't care. But, be sure of one thing, I've worn them all out so, don't you go thinking that you can use them to torment some poor pilgrim coming behind me!"

I opened the box, took out a large bag, and sat it on the ground. I said, "See here, Devil, these are all the physical pains I suffered during my short life span. My God said you're responsible for them.

"So, I thought it only fitting that I should return them to you before I leave here. Among them, you'll find the pain of a heart attack, patched up arteries, disease ridden lungs, and years of struggling to get my breath.

"This next bag contains all the brokenness that tore my heart and mind when your old friend, Death snuck in and stole away my dear loved ones and left me alone. He took my wife, my son, and many of my dear friends. Yes, he took them all. Oh, but, I know where they are, and I'm on my way to be with them. In fact, we're going to have a grand reunion in a little while, and you're not invited! Then, there's the many times you stood against me when I preached the Word of God to all those lost souls on their way to hell. Oh, but, praise God some of them saw the light, and they're now safe with the Lord."

When I opened the third bag, a vile stench permeated the riverside. I said, "You will especially like this one, Devil. These are all the temptations and stumbling stones, and road blocks you placed in my pathway on my journey through this life. Do you remember the many times you tried to make me lose faith, and deny my precious Lord Jesus? And, when I had to climb that mountain, you cursed and threw stones at me. You yelled, 'Give it up! It's not worth it. God don't love you anymore.' Oh, but it was worth it, and you were wrong, as always.

"Now, my journey is over. My home is on the other side of that river. I can see the lights, and hear the sweet music, and Jesus is waiting for me. In fact, he's calling my name.

"You see, you been exposed, Devil. My Lord said that you are a 'liar.' He also said, 'Greater love hath no man than this, that he lay down his life for a friend.' He laid down his life for me on Calvary's rugged old cross where he bruised your head, and opened up a fountain of blood to wash my sins away. Yes, the Lamb of God sacrificed himself for me. He is my dearest friend. And, now my Father is calling, and I'm going home to be with him.

So, Devil, I leave all this to you, and I hope they add to your torment throughout all eternity while I bask in the awesome love of my God!"

If I Could Give Christmas to You

What a beautiful thought I am thinking;
'tis an honor and privilege too.
From a heart filled with love, I'd be giving,
if I could give Christmas to you.

I would grant that your heart would not be
ever broken by a heart that's untrue.
No pain would you have, no deep misery
if I could give Christmas to you.

With stardust, I'd fill you a coffer.
I would lift it right out of the blue.
Great jewels from heaven I would offer,
if I could give Christmas to you.

But, the pleasures of a man cannot be
to offer such treasures to you.
For Jesus was born of the Virgin Mary,
And God gave Christmas to you.

If I could give Christmas to you,
what a wonderful thing I would do.
I would take all your sorrows,
and fill your tomorrows,
if I could give Christmas to you.

Freedom Flashes
An Old Soldier's Talk With God About Old Glory

The old soldier threw his *Daily News* into the garbage can.
His eyes moved towards the rising sun, and he raised a trembling hand.
A tear-drop trickled down his cheek into his snow-white beard.
When he finally spoke, it was clear to me that God had tuned his ear.
"My Father," he said in a trembling voice, "I've passed the years of my prime.
I'm way on past the three score and ten of man's allotted time.
I watched a brand new century turn way back down the road.
When I see the way my country is headed, it bows me down so low.
Times have changed, and many things seem so out of place.
These old bones are tired, my strength is gone, and I can't keep up the pace.
When I read the news from day to day, Sir, I just can't help but wonder;
The lifeless age that haunts these bones; has it happened to our country?
Our fathers forged a plan and launched this nation on the road to liberty.
They laid its roots in the Word of God with the idea that all men should be free.
Black marble stones are a monument to that son of mine who died,
With many others in Vietnam. What a godless place to give their lives.
Just this morning in the paper, Sir, I read an awful story.
The high court of our nation ruled that it's all right for some folks to burn
Old Glory.
Why, old glory stood in the court house, Sir, where the deeds of men were tried.
She waved proud on the battlefield where our brave soldiers died.
Now she lays on our city streets trampled 'neath the feet of men;
Men not worthy of one drop of blood spilled by our fighting men.
To her stars and stripes some set a flame and turn her colors to ashes,
And as those flames leap up to you, I wonder will there be nothing left but
freedom flashes?
How many graves must yet be filled? How many hearts must be broken?
How many eyes must be washed with tears, before men stop their killing?
In the Holy Book, I read about a time when war won't even be a memory.
What a glorious day when Jesus reigns, and all men will truly be free.
Until that wonderful day arrives, My Father, my prayer is this:
Raise up Godly leaders, Sir, to steer this nation through the roughest seas.
And let Old Glory keep on waving over the land of the brave and the free.
Amen!

THE OCEANS ARE THE TEARDROPS

God spread his mighty arms as far as his eyes could see.
He walked across the vastness, and called it eternity.
He flung the stars across the universe, and hung the worlds in space.
By the power of his word, he made a trail for the Milky Way.

He made the earth from nothing, then he held it in his hand.
He scooped out the ocean floors, and made the mountains grand.
He piled up a handful of stones near the eastern sea
Shaped it like a skull, and called it Calvary.

He designed a rugged cross where his precious Son would die
To pay the awful price for the sinner such as I.
He sent his Son named Jesus as our sacrificial lamb.
From the cross on Calvary's Hill, he saved this sinful man.

The oceans are the teardrops God shed at Calvary
As his hands made the cross where Jesus died for me.
His fingers drew the blueprint that would set my spirit free.
The oceans are the teardrops God shed at Calvary.

THERE'S A SHADOW IN THE VALLEY

There's a valley called death near the river of life
Where the ending of time awaits you and I.
God has appointed that each one shall go
To lay down the treasures he's gathered below.

His gold and his silver, and all of earth's stones
Will fade like the sunset, their beauty be gone.
When I reach that valley, I won't be alone,
For Jesus is waiting to carry me home.

To the valley called Death, came Jesus one day,
And the giver of life tore death's sting away.
He unlocked the doors to death's prison walls.
And, he carried its keys to the kingdom of God.

When you reach that valley, look for a stone,
Set there by Jesus when the battle was won.
These words are inscribed by the finger of Him,
"There's only a shadow where death once has been."

There's a shadow in The Valley
Where death used to be,
And I know my Redeemer
is waiting for me.

There's nothing to fear now,
No fears will there be.
There's a shadow in The Valley
Where death used to be.

Crossing Jordan

Somewhere, there's a river that I must cross one day;
A place they call Jordan, where this life slips away.
Safe in the arms of Jesus free from danger and harm,
I'll cross chilly Jordan to my heavenly home.

When I'm crossing Jordan, the Lord will hold my hand.
I'll be taking flight to the promised land.
He'll be right beside me, it's all in God's plan.
When I'm crossing Jordan, the Lord will hold my hand.

When you come to Jordan, remember what you're told
The waters of that river run swift, and they're cold.
A man cannot swim it, Jesus made a better way.
With Jesus there to guide us, we'll fly away!

HE'S ALWAYS READY

God put a king out in the field.
For seven long years, he ate with the deer.
When God finally raised him from the ground,
The king had no doubt, God wore the crown.

God found old Jonah asleep in the boat.
He told the sailors, "See if he floats."
When the fish spat old Jonah out on the sand,
He knew for sure that God can save a man.

God told a preacher, "There's a sale on down town."
To the auction he came, and laid his money down.
The purchase he made was part of his life.
The slave that he bought was Gomer, his wife.

God left his home on Zion's holy hill.
In the Garden one night, he gave up his will.
He laid down his life, and took it up again,
To pay the awful price for the sins of men.

My God has power to do anything.
He speaks like thunder, and makes the heavens ring.
His lightening flashes across the sky.
He's always ready to help you and I.

TAKE ME BACK

There's an old country church house standing high upon a hill,
Where I first met up with Jesus, and he broke my stubborn will;
Where the saints of God all gathered 'round each Sabbath Day and prayed,
For the Lord to touch this sinner boy, and change his wicked ways.

Somewhere on that hillside, where the little church house stands,
There's a grave that has no tombstone, or the name of any man.
In the grave, there lies the bones of a sinner now set free;
Freed one Sunday night by the Man from Galilee.

Take me back to that old altar where I knelt one day and prayed.;
Where the blood of Jesus cleansed me and washed my sins away.
On my knees, there let me linger. Let me breathe his holy name,
Until he reaches down and touches me, and fills my soul again.

THE BABY WHO LAY IN THE HAY

If God, in his infinite, wonderful mind,
Should allow this pilgrim to go back in time;
And if I could chose anywhere I could be,
On the hill with the shepherds, I'd hear the angels sing.

For the angels did sing a heavenly hymn.
They sung "Peace on earth good will to men."
They told of a king who had come to earth.
"He was born," they said, "by a miracle birth."
He would walk among men, and show them the way.
They told of a baby who lay in the hay.

If God should allow me to go back and stand
By some blessed old relic remembered by man,
And if I could choose anywhere I could be,
I would stand by the manger 'till he smiled upon me.

The babe in the manger was God's little lamb
Destined to die for the sins of all men.
Thirty years he would walk upon this earth.
Many lives he would change by a miracle birth.
On an old rugged cross, he would die one day,
This precious little baby who lay in the hay.

If God, in his generous, marvelous grace,
Should allow this sinner to take another man's place,
And if I could chose anyone I could be,
I would trade with old Simon. I would carry the tree.

The baby who gave sweet Mary such a thrill,
One day would walk up Calvary's Hill.
He would carry my sins, and never once groan,
'Till the load grew so heavy he couldn't go on.
He would light up my life, and show me God's way,
This precious little baby who lay in the hay.

BEGGAR FROM THE EARTH

This story begins in a mansion on a hill;
A poor man's paradise where a wealthy merchant lived.
He had all of earth's treasures his mansion could hold.
But, his heart was empty, it was just a black hole.

For the light of God's love had never shown
Deep in his dark soul where love should have grown.
Through all the years, he dwelt on this earth,
He had never discovered his dear brother's worth.

God gave the rich man all the things that caught his eye.
They belonged to him until the day that he died.
God would never force him to give them away.
But, God laid a beggar by the rich man's gate.

Not one little piece of this world would he give.
Poor Lazarus asked for nothing but a crumb of bread.
The rich man would not be a poor beggar's friend.
In hell, he begs for water, and calls out Lazarus's name.

When the rich man looked out through the flames of hell,
In Abraham's bosom, he could see old Lazarus well.
The rich man had become a beggar in the flames.
The beggar from the earth was the son of The King.

PICKS AND SPADES

I don't talk about the things I did when I was doing sin.
In the sea of God's forgetfulness, Jesus buried them.
When he cast them in that blessed sea, all the host of heaven cheered.
He placed guards all around that pit so you can't go fishing there.

From the fiery pit of hell, the old Devil's buzzards come.
They feed on sins of the past, they just love to dig up bones.
In true old vulture style, they'll gather one by one.
They'll pick a carcass clean, and leave it drying in the sun.

You've got no right to trace my past, and search for the old man's grave
You've got no right to dig up sins that God himself forgave.
Jesus died to set us free, our sinful souls to save.
God gave us his precious Son, he didn't give us picks and spades.

Home

There's a place upon a mountain
Where I laid my wife to rest.
She went home to be with Jesus,
And left my heart in a broken mess.

Together we climbed life's tallest mountains
Where the howling winds chill the soul.
The valleys we crossed were dark and dangerous,
But we never gave up, we were going home.

There's a place on a holy mountain
Where we'll meet one glorious morn,
Free from heartaches, pain and sorrow.
We'll live with Jesus in our heavenly home.

Home is just a few miles journey
Somewhere over life's rolling sea.
She and Jesus will be waiting.
With open arms, they'll welcome me.

I Can Hear the Angels Sing

One night on a hill, near Bethlehem,
The angels sang a glorious hymn.
Through the halls of time, their message rings.
And, I can hear the angels sing.

One morning at a tomb, near Calvary,
From death's cold hand, Jesus rose free.
Eternal live He died to bring,
And I can hear the angels sing.

One night on my knees at an altar rail,
Jesus saved my soul from the fires of hell.
Since that day, my soul's been clean.
And, I can hear the angels sing.

I can hear the angels sing.
Oh, how they make the heavens ring!
They sing about a child who is a king.
And, I can hear the angels sing!

I Found a Place

Tell me who do you turn to when there's nobody there?
When your heart is so heavy your burdens you can't bear,
When the chilly hand of death wraps its fingers around your soul,
Who do you turn to, brother, where do you go?

When the storms of life are raging, and temptations around me roll,
I find my secret hide away, and bare my burdened soul.
King Jesus meets me on my knees, and drives away my fears.
He gives me peace and comfort, and wipes away my tears.

I found a place where I can go to find sweet healing for my soul.
And, I've never found the Devil hanging around.
I fall down on my knees, and cry, Dear Father, would you please?
And it pleases him to fill my every need.

I Just Can't Wait

I've been walking this road for many long years.
Had me some heartaches shed a lot of tears.
Devil tried to get me every time I've turned around.
Jesus has been walking right by my side.
He's been my comfort, he's been my guide.
Every time I found that I could not walk, he carried me.

I've just about made it to the other side.
I've been looking across Jordan for just a little while;
Listening to the music coming from a heavenly land.
Some day he'll call, and I'll fly away
To my home over yonder, and there I'll stay.
I'll shout up and down those streets of gold,
And praise God's name while the ages roll.

Oh, I just can't wait to step inside those pearly gates.
I just can't wait to see King Jesus face to face.
I just can't wait to see my Father on his throne,
And hear him say, "Well done, my child, welcome home."

I'VE BEEN DOWN THIS ROAD BEFORE

I've been down this road before. I don't want to go back again.
Sometimes I walk this road with my face down on my chin.
If I make it through the valley, just one more time,
There's one more mountain I'll have to climb.
I'll have to climb Mt. Pisgah's lonely hill.

When it seems all the trouble in the world is mine,
God gives me a picture of glory divine.
I see my Jesus hanging on Calvary's tree.
Then, I look across Jordan to my heavenly home.
I see him sitting in power on his throne,

JESUS CARRIES ME

Jesus holds my hand when I'm climbing up the mountain.
Jesus holds my hand when I'm walking by the sea.
Jesus holds my hand when I need someone to cling to.
When I'm in the valley, Jesus carries me.

Those foot prints in the valley belong to Jesus.
He left them there when he brought me through the trial.
He held me in his arms and carried me like a child.
Then he walked every step through my valley.

If you're headed for the valley, look for Jesus.
He'll be there when you reach the storm.
With a mighty hand he'll hold you in his tender arms he'll fold you.
When you're in the valley, he will carry you.

Once In A While, Now and Then

Once in a while my heart gets heavy.
Once in a while my teardrops flow.
Once in a while I get homesick.
Once in a while I gotta' go
Down to the alter where I met Jesus.
Once in a while my cup overflows.
Because
Now and then I get happy.
Now and then he touches my soul.
'Now and then I feel a moving.
Now and then the glory rolls
Down to the altar when I talk to Jesus.
Now and then he blesses my soul.

THE HAND ON THE TABLE

Jesus met his disciples for the Passover meal,
Longing for the moment his passion would be filled.
The time was at hand for salvation to be wrought.
Tender hands that broke the bread would be nailed to the cross,

Hands that touched the withered hand passed the cup around,
And when they reached for the bowl, the traitor was found.
With a towel and some water, Jesus fell to his knees.
Holy hands that made the man now washing his feet.

There's a hand on the table stained with silver and blood,
It's the blood of the Savior, Jesus, the Lamb of God.
Thirty pieces of silver were counted his worth.
He was sold to the Devil by the hand on the table.

THE HILLS OF ETERNITY

Coming across the hills from eternity,
I see God with a plan in his hand.
Oh, he's looking for a man,
For his life, he'll lay his down.

Coming up the hill towards Calvary,
I see a man with a crown on his head.
On his back, there's a cross.
By his side, a man who's lost.

Coming up the hill towards eternity,
I see a man, and he is the Son of God.
Oh, the cross he has laid down,
For the sinner he has found.

Coming across the hills of eternity,
I see a King riding on a white horse.
In his hand, there's a crown.
He'll give it to the man he's found.

THE NAILS

I met an old man with his head bowed low;
His shoulders were bent and his steps were slow.

There were tears in his eyes and, I thought, how sad,
To see an old man cry like a lad.,

I said, "Sir, for the years you've lived,
You ought to be glad that you're still here.

He said, "Son, I've worked with these hands of mine.
I swung the hammer that molded the iron.

I pumped the bellow 'till there was no dross,
For, I made the nails that nailed Jesus to the cross.

ABRAHAM'S CITY FAIR

I'm a great grandson of Abraham. I'm looking for a home;
A city over yonder not made with hands where I'll never roam.
'Tis a city of gold I've heard them say where sorrows come no more.
I'll be resting from my weary journey when my traveling days are o'er.

I've traveled all over this country looking for a place to stay,
And a well of living water that will take my thirst away.
I've filled my cup and had a little drink from every well I've seen.
But, all the water in this old world cannot satisfy me.

I'm traveling on towards heaven, Abraham's city fair.
'Gonna lay my burdens down when I enter there.
I've found not a thing in this old world to make me cease to roam.
I've a friend over yonder who gave his life, and bought me a heavenly home.

Broken Hearted People Are God's Specialty

Many people will retire to their chambers tonight,
They will fall asleep hurting. Nothing will be right.
In the morning, when they rise, they will see them all again;
The many broken pieces scattered all around.

Life's precious hours will be wasted tonight.
People searching for an answer, something to make life right.
They have tried all the vices Satan holds in his hands,
But, when the pleasure has ended, the pain is there again.

If there's a broken heart somewhere tonight,
Jesus can mend it, he can make life right.
He will take the broken pieces, in his tender, loving hands.
With love, he will mold them and make life whole again.

Broken hearted people are God's specialty;
Those who are wounded all who have a need.
Yes, Jesus knows how a broken heart feels.
With a broken heart, Jesus died on Calvary's Hill.

BEGGAR MAN'S GOLD

When I was the lad of a Christian, wandering through the fields,
I came upon a gold mine near the foot of Zion's Hill.
The glow that came from deep within just set my soul on fire.
To search out all its riches then, became my heart's desire.

I went into that gold mine, my eyes with wonder wide.
These words were etched into the wall, "I Am the bread of Life,"
Reflected in that mirrored gold, an image I could see,
A sinner bought by Jesus' blood. His grace had pardoned me.

I heard a voice then whisper, soft, but crystal clear,
"Dig into my Word, my Son, you'll find treasure there."
So, through those golden nuggets, I began to search around.
I tell you nothing can compare to the treasures I have found.

I knew among those nuggets lay a treasure I could hold.
I searched until I found it. It was shaped like Father's soul!
As I stuffed it in my pocket, I heard my Father say,
"Give it to a beggar, Son, when you meet him in the way."

I found a golden nugget down in my Father's mine.
The measure of its worth no treasure can you find.
I will keep this treasure, for it is mine to hold.
My Father gave it to the poor. His Word is beggar man's gold.

Gathering Home

Gathering home, they're gathering home.
All of my loved ones are leaving me alone.
They're gathering yonder on the hills of glory.
They're waiting for me to come and be with them.
Gathering home, they're gathering home.

One by one they're leaving this land of sorrow
for a land of love and a sweet tomorrow.
There's no more heartache, pain and tears,
no more sin, no death, no fears.
They're leaving here for a holy land

Jesus said, "I want you here with me."
He's calling those that he set free.
He freed them from this world of sin
when he shed his blood on Calvary's hill.
They're going there to be with him.

AT THE FOOT OF THE HILL

What an awful way for a man to die
On Calvary's hill, and I wonder why.
Why would he die for a wretch like me?
To forgive all my sins, and set me free.

How could he stand in the courts of man,
And place his life in their wicked hands?
How could he walk through the street in shame,
And let them mar his holy name?

What an awful thing it must have been
When God turned his face away from him.
When God turned and looked the other way,
'My God, why?" They heard Jesus say.

They placed him there in a cold, stone grave.
Three days and nights his body lay.
To the depths of hell, my Lord did go.
And, he conquered man's eternal foe.

On Sunday morning as the sun did rise,
The shades of death fell from his eyes.
An angel rolled the stone away.
At the foot of the hill, there's an empty grave.

RESURRECTION POWER

Standing by the graveside, I heard a distant rumble.
As it peeled across the heavens, I thought it was thunder.
Then the ground began to tremble, and I heard a trumpet sound.
All across the graveyard, folks were coming from the ground.

I felt resurrection power flowing all over me.
In less than a heartbeat, with Jesus I would be.
I felt resurrection power flowing through my bones.
In the twinkling of an eye, I will be gone.

This resurrection power is now lifting me,
Soon I will look into his eyes, my Jesus I will see.
He will take me to my heavenly home.
Good-bye old world! This pilgrim's gone!

SIMON, COME AND CARRY HIS CROSS

Simon, come and carry his cross.
Simon, come and carry his cross!
Just a few more steps to Calvary,
And we'll hang the Son of God.

I've walked many men down the road of death.
I've watched many people die.
But, I've never seen a man like him.
I've never looked into those eyes.

The poor folks say he is a preacher man.
Judas said he is a king.
Herod said he is the prophet John
Come back from the grave.

Peter says he is the Son of God.
He's the hope that cannot fail.
But, I guess it really doesn't matter now.
We're going to hang him with these nails.

I know he walked up Calvary's hill,
And hung there just for me.
He saved my soul from a devil's hell,
When his blood ran down that rugged old tree.

IF HE'LL BREAK THE BREAD

I sat at the table near my Father's right hand.
I ate of the food that came from his land.
I walked o'er the mountains that he called his own.
Many times now I wonder, why did I roam?

I wasted the money that he gave to me.
I spent it on pleasures, things I could see.
I walked down the highway that leads from his fold.
Many nights I remember, I slept in the cold.

Sometimes in the evening, when the shadows grow plain,
It seems I can hear him, he's calling my name.
He's coming, oh I know it, He's looking for me.
Oh, what will I tell him when his face I see?

I'll work for my wages, just a servant I'll be.
If he'll break the bread and bless it for me.

I'll Heal Your Broken, Bleeding Heart

Verse 1

I knelt by the road of life searching for the pieces
of my broken heart and shattered dreams scattered all around.
Through the glimmer of my tear drops, I cried, "Lord this can't be
How could you let it break apart through this tragedy?"

Chorus

He said, "Let me hold the pieces of your broken bleeding heart
I'll keep them all together. I won't lose one tiny part.
And when the time is ready, I'll join them once again.
With love, I'll truly heal your broken, bleeding heart.

Chorus

Verse 2

I left my roadside prayer room with loneliness and fear.
Down the road, I could see nothing to hold me here.
It's hard to see through bloody tears when your heart is torn.
"Lord, I beg you hold me close. I don't know how to be alone."

Verse 3

On this road with Jesus I am walking.
He carries my load and holds my trembling hand.
Now and then he whispers to me gently.
"Trust me, Child, this all fits my master plan."

Chorus

Lyrics and tune by
Arnold R, Faw

HOLD MY TREMBLING HEART

I've about had all I can stand of this world's sin and pain.
I've had my share of heartaches, Lord, you know I have been tried.
Sometimes late at night, when I'm about to come unglued,
It scares me half to death when I think about what I might do.

Sometimes my heart gets shaky, I think it's out of control.
If it wasn't for your power, old Satan would have my soul.
It's then I need a sure anchor, I find it in your word.
"Greater is he that is in you, than he that is in the world."

Lord, you surely promised if I'd hold your nail scarred hand,
You'd take me through this sinful world to that promised land.
When I think I've done my best, and temptations around me loom,
Satan tries to use sin to pry my fingers loose.
When I feel I've lost my grip, and I can't hold to thee,
The hand that cannot let me go, was nailed to Calvary's tree.

Hold my trembling heart, Lord, keep me near thy throne.
I've a few more miles to travel before I reach my home.
I'm afraid that I might stumble, and fall down by the way.
When I reach that holy city, my trembling heart will be safe.

This is a song that I wrote for Lynn Pugh, on March, 29, 1998.
In 2002, she became my wife.
This song is available on CD. Please contact me for information.

He Knows the Trail

Many years I struggled on
through this world all alone.
Jesus knew I couldn't make it by myself.
On Calvary's hill, he took my hand
we're headed for the promised land.
He knows the trail all the way from the cross.

With the valley behind me
there's a mountain up ahead.
And I know that I'm not able to make the climb.
Jesus brought me through the valley,
and he'll help me climb the mountain.
He knows the trail all the way to the top.

He made a trail for you and me
through the fire and on the sea.
I see his footprints every step of the way.
Soon he's coming for his own,
he'll take us to our heavenly home.
We'll ride the clouds all the way to glory land.

I'm Gonna Be Changed

Some morning when you see me,
Brother, I'm gonna be changed.
I'll be just like my Savior.
I'll come out from the grave.

In the twinkling of an eye,
I'll lay this body down.
On the plains of Paradise,
I'll hold his nail scarred hand.

Changed I'm gonna be.
From sin, I will be free.
I'll wear his holy name,
Because I have been changed.

SOMEBODY WAITS FOR ME

I've lost everything this world has to offer. I've nothing that you can see.
According to its standards, I'm nothing but a beggar living in misery.
But, I've got a treasure that doesn't look like money laid up waiting for me.
And, the thought I carry as I make this journey, somebody waits **for** me.

The gates of pearl and the streets of gold gotta' be a sight to see.
And, the sweet, sweet fruit from the Tree of Life must be a heavenly treat.
But, I have a longing to see King Jesus, who died to set me free.
And the thought I carry as I make this journey, he's coming back for me.

"Sold!"

How much would you give me?" Cried the auctioneer that day;
"For this broken down old prostitute?" And, then he laughed,
"Why she would still make a good slave."

From the back of the crowd, there raised the hand
Of a gray haired, old preacher man.
"Two sheckels I'll give," in a trembling voice he cried.

Then someone bid three, and another offered five.
The auctioneer shook his head and cursed beneath his breath.
"I should have been a tax collector at this rate, I may starve to death,"

He pumped the bidding, and the crowd began to cheer.
They all grew quiet when the old preacher approached the auctioneer.
"Fifteen sheckels of silver I'll give. That's all I could find."

The auctioneer shook his head and sneered at the old preacher.
"Why, that's not enough money to buy this lovely creature."
Tears ran down the old preacher's cheeks, "I'll give a homer and half of
barley wheat."

"Maybe I'll take your price," said the old slave seller.
"But, I'd like to know why. I wonder, would you tell us?"
What would an old man such as you do with a broken down, worn out
prostitute?"

"Why she can keep house and cook and sew too. You see, she's the mother
of Amy and Ru.
We'll grow old as we share a life. Her name is Gomer, Sir, she's my wife."

 Fifteen sheckels of silver, and two and one half bushels of dog food was
the price Hosea paid for Gomer his wife.

I Thought I'd Seen It All

I've seen a wonderous sight as I've walked upon this earth.
I've seen a flower bloom. I've seen a baby's birth.
I've seen a star fall from its place, and streak across the sky.
I've seen lightening kill a man. It made me wonder why.

I've seen the great Nor-Eastern blow, and raise the ocean tide.
I've seen a father give his life, because his children cried.
I've seen stardust fall to earth that came from the milky way.
I've seen mighty men brought down and laid within the grave.

I thought I'd seen it all until I walked up Calvary's Hill.
There I saw a man whose blood the soldiers spilled.
I thought I'd heard it all until I heard him say,
"Yes, he's guilty, God, forgive his sins today."
I saw him hanging there, and I saw the life he gave.
I thought I'd seen it all until I saw that empty grave.

THIS HOUSE I'M LIVING IN

This old house I'm living in will soon be falling down.
Nothing that I know of will make it safe and sound.
The paint has faded on its walls, the windows cracked and breezy.
When the final moment comes, I hope she goes down easy.

It's been my home for many years, but the time is near for leaving.
She'll turn to dust when I'm gone, but this old soul won't be grieving.
There's a robe of white awaiting me like the one that Jesus wears.
Free from heartache, grief and pain, and all these worldly cares.

I'll leave the things behind that caused this house to fall,
And, move on over to glory land when King Jesus calls.
The robe he'll wrap this poor soul in will last eternally,
In the presence of the one I love, who gave his life for me.

You Won't Hear His Footsteps

As the people crowded into the store, a gentleman stepped out of line and came up to me. He stuffed a folded paper into my hands, smiled and said, "This is just for you."

I put it in my pocket and finished my chores. When the all the customers had been waited on, I took the paper out, unfolded it and read the only line written on the page. It said, "If you listen closely, you can almost hear the footsteps of Messiah."

I turned and called to the cashier behind me, Hey, find that fellow and bring him back here. I've read the Book, and I want to tell him what John said!

He won't be walking down the pathway.
You won't hear his footsteps on the pavement.
You won't see him on the TV.
He won't call you on the phone.
He'll call us from the clouds of glory,
he'll take God's children home.
And, we'll be gone! Yes, we'll be gone!

Before he left this world, Jesus told the ones he loved.
Don't let your hearts be troubled, believe the words I say.
I'm going to my Father's land and build a home for you.
And, when it's finished, I'll return and take you home with me.

THE JOURNEY HOME

Reaching for the door knob, wondering what I will find,
Is she still waiting for me, or am I left behind?
This awful thing that is taking her came from the pit of hell.
And, I can tell you, my friend, it has done its job so well.
I have watched her body slowly disappear.
Soon she will be gone, and I will face my greatest fear.

I do not know how to be alone, we've been one for so long.
This was not the plan when we began our journey home.
So many things we hoped to do must now be cast aside.
What will I do when she is gone, no longer by my side?
The road of life is long and hard, it takes its toll on you and me.
Life's events will make us strong, or do us in, you see.

Almighty God said that, it's not good for man to be alone.
So, God made a help meet to walk beside him as he journeys on.
We have shared our load, our laughter, our grief and fears.
Her journey will soon be over, and God will wipe away her tears.
If I hold the hand of Jesus, I will never be alone.
Lord, help me not to stumble on my way to our new home.

A Song for My Friend

From the other side of the table, he looked at me and grinned.
And, he talked about how blessed he was just to call me his friend.
Then he said, "I'll tell you Brother, I just can't help but wonder
Why the Lord has brought our paths so close to him."

As we ate our food together, we talked about our lives.
We talked about how hard it is sometimes just to smile.
And, when our conversation touched on God's relation,
I saw the image of our Father in his eyes.

I knew that God had sent him to help me with this load.
For the path that I had walked upon, had been a lonesome road.
My feet sometimes had stumbled, my spirit too had crumbled,
For, a man cannot bear his cross alone.

We talked on through the evening 'till the day was almost gone.
We knew that we'd be parting soon to make our journey home.
Then some day, over yonder when our feet have ceased to wonder,
Two friends will meet again at God's heavenly throne.

Oh, what a day that's going to be
When two old friends again shall meet.
When we gather on that heavenly shore,
We'll be together for ever more.

THE GRAY-HAIRED PREACHER MAN

He came down from the mountain many long years ago.
What little bit of hair he had was almost white as snow.
He carried a little black book, said it was the Word of God
From the way he walked, and the things he said,
He must have been where the angels trod.

He lived for years among us a poor, old, simple man.
He'd open up that Bible, and prove he was a wealthy man.
He told of a home over yonder where streets are paved with gold;
Where the tree of life forever blooms, and man won't ever grow old.

On a bright, Sunday afternoon, we laid his soul to rest.
That precious old black Bible was placed upon his chest.
As I stood there by his coffin, and thought about God's plan,
Oh, it wouldn't be right to bury that Book in the box with the preacher man.

He could preach God's Word about the best I've ever heard,
And I've heard many preachers.
When he preached about love, it fell from above, it lifted the sinful creature.
It thrilled my soul to hear the story told by the gray-haired preacher man.
He did a mighty good job with the Word of God, he spread it all over this land.

THE STRANGER IN THE PEW

Not a sound could there be heard
As the old gentleman came down the street.
Strange, I thought, as I watched him there.
You should at least hear the shuffle of his feet.

Like a master, sure, he carried himself,
And his eyes, they were not dimmed.
Then something stirred inside of me,
And I felt as if I had always known him!

He went inside and sat himself
Down near the center aisle.
And, when we sang "Amazing Grace,"
There crossed his face a smile.

I wondered who he might be,
This stranger in our meeting.
But, when the Reverend took the stand,
I knew, he came to hear the preaching!

The preacher read from God's own word
The way of life for sinners.
Then preached about the love of One
Who died to make men winners.

The snow-haired man sat quiet and still,
And gave his full attention.
While every word that preacher spoke
Gave to Him a full dimension!

I saw a tear drop from his cheek,
And fall down on "The Book."
Where that tear drop found its place,
I sure would like to look.

"Old Man," I said when we stepped outside,
"We're glad you came our way."
"Oh, I wouldn't have missed it for the world," he said.
"My daughter preached here today."

Then back inside that church I ran
To catch one final view.
From the glow that lingered there, I had no doubt.
My Heavenly Father had occupied that pew!

To my pastor, Linda Greene, for Pastor Appreciation Sunday, 1/10/87
Arnold R. Faw

To My Wife on our Twenty-Fifth Wedding Anniversary

Almost bewildered, the angel said, "Sir, these orders aren't quite clear."
"What seems to be the problem?" he said. "All vital statistics are here."

"I know, Sir," the angel did agree, "He's been my charge for years.
I've watched him through most everything, and caught a bucket full of tears.

If it could be done by mortal man, Sir, I do believe;
When I had to ride that Ford with him, he scared eternity out of me.

I watched him as he learned to walk, and helped him get about,
Then chased him through the woods each day, and heard his dirty mouth.

Sir, I don't mind the hardest task, but the chances now are slim,
Why, it would take a miracle, Sir, to find a bride for him.

He would want her young and pretty too. She must have vim and vigor.
'Twould be so hard to find her, Sir. She would have so much to do.

He might pick at her and laugh sometimes when her heart grew very tender.
And, if she didn't truly love him, Sir, I'm sure it would offend her.

He'd forget to say, I love you, dear when she needed it the most,
He forgets to eat his breakfast, Sir, he can't remember toast.

There is no one that I can think who would take on such a task.
She would have to be your daughter, Sir, do anything you ask.

Her name, I know, he would surely change. He would call her by his own."
The Lord just smiled at him and said, "Go talk to Linda Draughn."

12/24/85

I Won't Miss Him

He placed the last rose upon the casket.
He bowed his head, he grinned, and I heard him sigh.
This old world will be a better place without him.
No longer must we hear his sinful lies.

He climbed the ladder of success day by day.
He filled his life with all his wealth had brought.
He would not be a good friend to his brother.
There'll be no music played when his song is sung.

From the top of the hill, today he tumbled.
He's gone the way all mortal men must trod.
He left his wealth down here for others.
I wonder what he said when he met my God.

He's gone, and I'm glad, and I won't miss him.
I hope I live until I see these memories healed.
Down inside, there's a part of me that wonders,
What did he see when he climbed up over death's hill?

Joshua Paul Harris

In the likeness of our savior, God above has surely made you.
Just a tiny, precious thing fashioned by the King of Kings.
A jewel from heaven God has given to Mike and Judy for their blessing.
Within their hands, they will rub and mold until the gleam is purest gold.
With kind and gentle, loving hands they will teach how to be a man.
And, when this manhood you shall witness, be about your Father's business.

DADDY'S GIFT

Daddy crossed that Jordan River
Early one Christmas morn.
Many years down here he wandered
Looking for his heavenly home.
On the banks of the raging river,
The angels gathered there
To carry him over death's waters,
To his home so bright and fair.

On the other side of that river,
Daddy waited for Mom to come.
He knew that she would not linger,
Her race down here was won.
In the light of Heaven's glory,
Once again those two embraced.
They'll share heaven together,
And every day will be Christmas day!

What a gift God gave my Daddy,
To be in heaven on Christmas day.
Walking up and down those streets of gold,
His cares all passed away.
Singing with the angels, talking with Jesus,
Living in the heavenly way.
What a gift God gave my Daddy,
And it came on Christmas day!

GOD'S SOLDIER BOY

I'm walking down life's road with my sword in my hand.
My gun is in its holster, and Jesus holds my hand.
I carry many titles like "racist, homophobe, and clinger."
But the one that suits me best, the liberals refuse to mention.
I've been called a "Bible Thumper," and names not fit to whisper;
but they won't call me Christian, because they hate Captain Jesus.

I'm a soldier on the battlefield, in the army of the Lord,
we're marching through to Zion's Hill on Jordan's eastern shore.
The battles have been tough, the wounds I've had are many,
but the scars on me are nothing compared to those of Jesus.
Scars of thorns lace his brow, scars of nails are in his hands.
A Roman whip scarred his back made it look like plowed up ground.

On a hill they call "The Skull," Captain Jesus hung upon a tree.
There he bled and died to set this sinner free.
He freed me from a life of sin, and the awful fires of hell.
No longer am I living under Satan's damning spell.
So I joined this holy army to battle for the souls of men
so they won't walk in darkness, and miss heaven in the end.

Up ahead there's a city where God's soldiers are gathering in.
It's a place of peace and joy, and love, and life will never end.
There is no hate, or weapons, or war, or killing in that land.
Death will never stalk its streets. He's been defeated by Jesus' mighty hand.
Many things we face down here will be missing in that place.
Those who hate my God are not allowed to bring disgrace.

There'll be no alter on which the liberals sacrifice our babies,
God will cast it into hell where it will receive its just earned wages.
No politician will tell us lies to get us to the polls.
God almighty runs that country, and only truth will there be told.
We're marching on till Jesus comes with heaven's mighty army,
and rids this earth of godless men who spread hate and bring disorder.

Soon I'll face life's final battle. I'll lay down my sword and gun.
I'll look back on this world of sorrow, and tell old Satan, "Thank God it's done."
It's been my pleasure to spar with you, do battle for my Lord.
He'll open wide the gates of glory, and welcome home his soldier boy.
This soldier's garb I'll lay aside, it has no place beyond this world of sin.
Only peace, and love and joy are waiting for those who enter in.

Perhaps he'll pin some medals on my robe of white.
The victor's crown I' know I'll wear, Jesus gave me the right.
There is a mansion awaiting me built by The Carpenter's hand,
somewhere near the River of Life over in Glory Land.
But the thing I'm mostly longing for is to hear Captain Jesus say,
"Well done my faithful soldier boy, come on in and stay."

MISS LOTTYS GONE

Somewhere inside of paradise
On heaven's golden hills,
Miss Lotty met with Jesus
The keeper of her will.

His arms were wide extended.
His face set in a smile.
His voice like thunder, pealed through heaven,
"Welcome home my faithful child."

The Tolbert clan had gathered 'round
The gates of life eternal
To welcome home this faithful one
Who, for so long had journeyed.

The road of life she tread upon
Was graced with prints of Jesus.
On another road with other prints,
The world would never see her.

On this side of Jordan's banks,
Her friends and loved ones gathered.
Through tears of loss and shouts of praise
We waved good bye, but not forever.

When my journey here is o'er,
I'll hear that call from home.
I'll bid farewell to this old world,
Then I shall go where Lotty has gone.

In Loving Memory of Ambassador Chris Stevens, Officer Sean Smith, CIA Operatives, Glenherty and Tyrone Woods

Bengazi is a story the liberals don't want told.
It's the story of two leaders with hearts as black as coal,
And four brave men who died so others could go free.
They faced an evil foe, and paid the price of liberty.

President Obama and his Secretary, Wicked Hillary was her name,
Lied about what happened, on a movie, they laid the blame.
In the comfort of their office, they listened as the battle raged
As three brave soldiers in Bengazi stood against hell ablaze.

The hours dragged on by, and the soldiers stood their ground.
But, Hillary and Obama gave the orders to, "Stand down!"
The ultimate price was paid by three brave soldier boys,
Because Hillary and Obama would not offend the Muslim lords.

They seized our Ambassador, and beat him mercilessly.
They dragged him from the Compound, and left him dying in the street.
Abandoned by the one who chose him to represent America afar,
He died for the cause of freedom, and showed the world who we really are.

Some day without a warning, this story may rearrange,
And two souls as black as coal may go walking through the flames.
Bengazi was a horrible moment, but hell is eternity
For those whose hatred for others prevents men from being free.

1/23/20

THE CALL I DIDN'T GET

I don't know his name, and we never met,
But he answered the call that I didn't get.
He left his home, his family and friends,
And went over seas, our freedom to defend.

He slept in a hole dug in the mud.
Someday, he knew, it would soak up his blood.
He slept very little, and ate from a tin.
Keeping the watch was important to him.

He watched his buddies fall like leaves.
This manmade hell brought him to his knees.
There he met Jesus, who answered his call,
Who surely would catch him, if, he should fall.

He faced the enemy, and showed no fear.
When the battle grew hot, he was always there.
He was hard as a rock and strong as a lion.
But, when a buddy fell, he'd be a crying.

He stood tall and strong and never gave in,
But that bullet in his chest made quick his end.
I salute this hero who had the grits
To answer the call that I didn't get.

When I think of him, I'm reminded of Jesus.
He gave up heaven just to come and save us.
The soldier gave his life in an earthly hell.
Jesus gave his life to save us from hell.

He gave up heaven so holy and pure,
And came down to earth sin's curse to cure.
He slept in a boat, and walked on the sea.
He healed the sick, raised the dead, and set men free.

He saved my soul from the curse of sin.
He opened up heaven so I could come in.
On the battlefield, on Calvary's hill,
Jesus answered the call that I never will.

The call has gone out. There's a place up ahead,
Where everyone must go to settle up his debt.
Jesus knew that I couldn't, so over on Calvary's Hill,
He answered the call that I never will.

SILVER THREADS

With silver threads, God sewed up all the years of our life.
He stitched them all together through heartaches, tears and strife.
When the troubles of this world tore our world apart,
I wondered if those stitches could mend a broken heart.

He sewed some years with laughter, some he sewed with joy.
Now and then, he laced a year with sorrow's bitter cord.
With a careful hand of love, he stitched each year in place.
When the road grew dark and dangerous, He gave us traveling grace.

Now the silver years are gone, the trophy here we hold.
We're pressing on together. We're looking for the gold.
If the threads of time unravel, before we hold it in our hands,
He'll bring us back together with gold in glory land.

God sewed our years together with the silver thread of time.
As we walk along life's road, we can feel his hand in ours.
As we hold on to each other, and travel on as one,
That silver thread is turning gold, and we're on our journey home.

This is a song I wrote to my wife, Linda Draughn in honor of our twenty-fifth wedding anniversary. The song is available on CD.
Please contact me for information.

Swiftly Gone

Our Christmas wreath came from the funeral home this year;
A tall, white-haired man came and placed it there.

He asked none of us to give our permission;
Just the look on his face told of his mission.,

More bold than a thief the death angel appeared,
When the first rays of morning broke over the hills.

So suddenly he came and so swiftly he was gone,
Not even a "good-bye" was whispered in our home.

My brother was taken in the prime of his life;
He had no children, not even a wife.

The sweet wine of life he never had tasted,
Not a moment of time had he 'er wasted.

My heart is torn, wounded, and bleeding,
I wish I could show you the pain that I'm feeling.

But, with sweet assurance, I will pen every line,
To the lasting memory of this friend of mine.

To My Friend

He is, today, where the righteous stand,
The angels came and took his hand.
They led him across the Jordan wide,
For him there was no chilling tide,

I'll miss his presence here below,
But, he's better off by far, I know.
The cares of life he left behind,
No more hills he'll have to climb.

He lived his life in touch with God,
The path of sin he would not trod.
He made a vow when but a boy,
To keep his eyes upon the Lord.

For thirty years he kept that vow,
To the god of "things" he did not bow.
His thoughts were filled with another dimension,
Somewhere beyond the stars, he mentioned.

He mined yellow gold from beneath the sod,
But, even that couldn't turn him from God.
With a heart more pure than the gold he found.
He met his maker on solid ground.

He left behind the things I need,
To help me through this time of grief.
Because his future I know was sealed,
One Sabbath day at Calvary's Hill.

So, I won't weep because he's gone,
His place is now in heaven's throng.
The love he gave us here below,
Is worth its weight in heaven's gold.

And, so it is with such sweet sorrow,
We part our ways until tomorrow,
When the trumpet sounds and the dead shall rise,
I'll meet him yonder in the skies.

In loving memory of Edwin Lionel Johnson,
who swiftly left for glory on, December 20, 1986.
Written by his brother-in-law, Arnold R. Faw.
Poem started December 20, 1986; completed 1-17

An Ode to Old Pony

I souped up Grandma's Pontiac, but I didn't let her know!
I bored it out and shaved its heads. Man, that Pony could go!
I parked it in the driveway left it on the gravel.
When Grandma felt the urge to ramble, Old Pony was ready to travel.
Yeah, I souped up Grandma's Pontiac, but I didn't let her know!

When Grandma fired it up, you should have heard her rumble.
She slammed the pedal to the metal, and Old Pony roared like thunder.
Grandma never heard Old Pony sound so wild before.
She put that shifter down to "D," and down the drive she tore.
Yeah, I souped up Grandma's Pontiac, but I didn't let her know!

Gravel rained like falling hail. What an awesome sight to see.
Oh! I thank God that I was hiding behind that big oak tree!
Old Pony screamed onto the highway burning rubber making smoke.
Grandma screamed as she crossed the road, "Honey, this ain't no joke!"
Yeah, I souped up Grandma's Pontiac but I didn't let her know!

Back and forth across the highway, Old Pony laid some tracks,
With Grandma fighting all the way trying to hold Old Pony back.
When she finally got her straightened up, Old Pony lit up like a rocket.
I thought, If Grandma does return, she'll stuff Old Pony in my back pocket!
Yeah, I souped up Grandma's Pontiac. I think I should have told her so!

Grandma and Old Pony were gone for a long, long time.
I got to thinking, if they don't return, I might just lose my mind.
Then I saw her coming down the road. Old Pony was in the wind.
When she flew by me, Grandma's face was covered with a great big grin.
Yeah, I souped up Grandma's Pontiac, and she found it out on the go!

Grandma rode Old Pony into the driveway not a gravel 'neath her tires,
I thought, what Grandma's about to say is 'gonna burn my ears like fire!
Grandma parked Old Pony, and straightened her britches up.
Would you believe when she walked by me, she gave me two thumbs up!
Yeah, I souped up Grandma's Pontiac, and she loves Old Pony so!

Now and then when she gets bored, Grandma gets that lead sled out.
She goes out to the country to stretch Old Pony out.
One day Grandma told me as we talked into the night,
"Honey, thank you for Old Pony, you fixed her up just right!"
Yeah, I souped up Grandma's Pontiac, and she loves to make Old Pony go!

When I've Talked About You

It's a cold, cloudy, rainy day. I'm feeling mighty blue;
Sitting here sad and lonely wondering what I'll do.
I think I'll call your new love, and let my mind run lose.
When I get his attention, I'm gonna talk about you.

I'll tell him how you captured me with your warm, tender smile.
I'll tell him how you loved me for just a little while.
I'll give him things to think about. I'll make him sick of you.
He'll know how you loved me when I've talked about you.

I'll tell him how you held me sometimes through the night.
I'll tell him how you kissed me in the pale moon light.
I'll fill his ears so full of you, he'll wish you'd never met.
And, when I've finished talking, he'll let you go, I'll bet.

I'll talk his danged old ears off, I'll go on and on.
When I hang this phone up, he'll want you gone.
If I hold on just a little longer, you'll come back to me,
'Cause when I've talked about you, he will set you free.

IN THE EARLY MORNING LIGHT

She laid down beside me sometime past midnight.
She put her loving arms around me and held me close and tight.
She whispered to me softly words I had not heard in years,
And we made love in my dreams in the early morning light.

We slipped across the border into another realm
Among those yellow roses where no one else had been.
As the morning light was breaking, we pledged our love again,
And we made love in my dreams in the early morning light.

It's been too many years since I held her in my arms.
It seems like yesterday I tasted her sweet charms.
Now dreams and memories fill my lonely nights,
And we made love in my dreams in the early morning light.

One day I'll walk that pathway that she took long ago.
We'll meet among those roses where love like a river flows.
Never again will our hearts be broken, and tears won't fill our eyes,
And we'll be together forever in love's sweet paradise.

LOVE BUG ITCH

I tried everything that I could think of
To get that little girl's mind on love.
She can sing like a bird, and cook good stew,
And play croquet, but she won't pitch woo.

I was about to give up, and sing the blues.
Then I made her an offer she couldn't refuse.
I've got a big Dodge Ram, and a little bit of cash,
And a love bug itch that ain't been scratched.

I'll take her down to Carolina beach.
We'll shift a little sand with our feet.
We'll skinny dip in the waters cool.
She'll get the itch, and we'll pitch a little woo.

GRANDPA AND THE PREACHER

Grandpa sat quietly drinking in the beauty of God's creation all around him. The pastor drove up got, out and sat down beside the old man. They talked about Jesus, the beautiful flowers, heaven and so much more. Then the preacher said, "Grandpa, what's your favorite time of year?" Grandpa's furrowed brow grew more wrinkled, his eyes grew misty, and as he spoke his lips began to quiver.

He said, "Well Son, I can't pick a favorite time of the year. You see, they all hold precious memories for me. I suppose Christmas is a favorite for most people. And certainly it is for me. My Dad died on Christmas morning. Every time it comes around, I can't help but remember how much that big man loved us all. And I remember when I was little they thought I was going to die. Dad carried me in his arms all night, and prayed. God heard and answered my Daddy's prayers.

Mother's Day would have to be a favorite. For, God called Mama home at Mother's Day. Yeah, she went home to be with Daddy and Jesus. just slipped away quietly in in her sleep. I found her that morning with her hand lifted up and her finger pointing towards heaven. There was a smile on her face, and I knew she and Dad were together again. When Mother's Day comes around I'm reminded that I had the most loving, giving, and godly mother on earth.

Who could resist springtime when the flowers bloom? Surely that's a gorgeous time when new life springs up everywhere. You see, the death angel came by again. This time he took my dear wife of thirty-two years. We built a life, raised a family, and had some good times, and some ups and downs. But, I won't linger here. For, there's another favorite time for me.

In the autumn, when the leaves begin to fall, my only son died. And now, it seems to me that I've given about all a man ought to give. But we never know what the future holds, or, who'll be the next one to answer the call. Perhaps it will be me, and that will be my favorite time of the year; when I can sweep through those pearly gates and once again embrace every one of them as the circle grows larger every day.

ONE MORE TIME

When we said good-bye and parted,
I grinned as I walked away.
I thought it really didn 't matter.
I'd find a new love right away.

I searched for love everywhere,
But my life just fell apart.
I found love all around me,
But love couldn't find my heart.

A man can lose most everything,
And make a brand new start.
If he is to live in this old world,
He'd better not lose his heart.

I came here just to see you one more time.
I've been wondering if I left something behind.
I'm looking for my heart, and a little peace of mind.
Yes, I came here just to see you one more time.

Bubba's Sweet Christmas

The ink was smeared on the tear stained lines of the letter that Santa read.
"Dear Santa Claus, I almost lied and told you my name is Fred.
But, you have ways of finding out who gets into trouble.
So, I'll just tell you right up front, you know me as 'Bubba.'

The story I'm about to tell you, Sir, may be hard to believe.
But, the trouble I'm in is not my fault, Mama brought it all on me.
I was a good little boy. I kept my cool, and I shunned all the evil I could see.
And, I did all right until last week when Mama bought the Christmas tree.

It took three men to set that thing on our living room floor.
And, to a little boy's eyes it was higher than the eagles soar.
Then Mama put a great big candy cane on our Christmas tree
way up in the top where something else ought to be.

It would have been better if she had placed a star, or an angel way up there
But, a candy cane on the top of our tree? Why, Santa, it just ain't fair!
It was red in the middle with yellow on the tip and white running through and through.
Slobber ran down my little fat lips. I tell ya it dripped like honey dew!

Now, that tree musta been 'bout nine feet tall. I'm 'bout two feet seven.
So I stacked some chairs in front of that thing, and made my way towards heaven.
I put my trust in the angels, Sir, I hear they hold them ladders well.
But, somewhere up that stack of chairs, my stinking ladder fell!

As my head went towards that knotty pine, I made one desperate swoop.
I latched on to that candy cane, and twirled like hula hoop!
Three times around that Christmas tree, and it began to come unglued.
When it turned me loose, around the room I sailed, then through the window
I flew!

To dig me outta that big snow bank, it took four men and a plow.
And, when I went inside, to my surprise, we had Christmas all over the house!
To say the least, I would not lie, Mama was mad as a hatter.
'Cause that Christmas tree looked as if a hurricane had made it scatter!

So, Santa Claus, don't be surprised when you get here Christmas eve,
if you find my little red butt hangin' on the Christmas tree!"

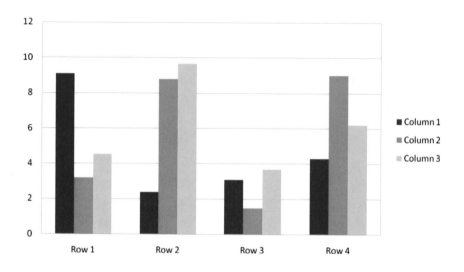

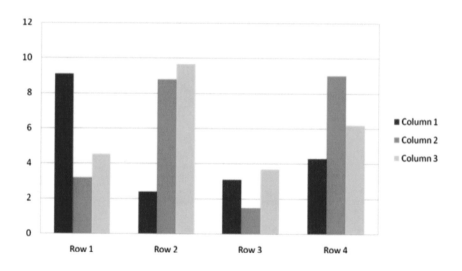